Facebook Marketing

ABOUT THE AUTHOR

George Pain is an entrepreneur, author and business consultant. He specializes in setting up online businesses from scratch, investment income strategies and global mobility solutions. He has built several businesses from the ground up and is excited to share his knowledge with readers.

DISCLAIMER

CONTENTS

BENEFITS OF FACEBOOK ADVERTISING?

With over 2.07 billion monthly active users, it is a no brainer that Facebook advertising provides an advertiser with a humongous outreach opportunity. It has certain unique advantages over other forms of advertising that makes Facebook advertising a must-have in any savvy advertiser's scheme of things. This may come as a surprise to many who think that online advertising begins and ends with Google. To them Facebook is merely a social media platform where you catch up with high school classmates and check out what your ex-flame is up to!

But the fact is that savvy marketers and advertisers are increasingly taking to Facebook advertising to market their products and services. The fact that Facebook earned a gargantuan $26 billion advertising revenue in 2017 is ample testimony. The benefits that accrue from Facebook advertising are quite significant and it is in a marketer's best interest to be fully conversant with them. Given below are the most important ones that every advertising and marketing professional worth his salt should know about-

1. **The Facebook Network-** Apart from Facebook itself, its affiliated social media platforms, Facebook Messenger and

Instagram boast of a fair amount of clout. Facebook Messenger with its one billion *very* active daily users. Instagram on the other hand has a creditable 600 million users, half of which follow some business account or the other!

Taken together the Facebook Network is a very formidable outreach medium, the like of which has never been seen before. The world over, people spend as much as 50 minutes a day on the Facebook network, which is truly incredible in terms of the outreach and engagement opportunity that it provides you. As a matter of fact, Facebook is accessed by 80% of all Internet users and there is no way that any advertiser can afford to not reckon with that kind of reach across demographic segments.

2. **Targeted Advertising-** Facebook advertising is as targeted as it can get. It enables advertisers to reach out to their precise target audience. That of course is just what marketers swear by as segmentation goes to the very root of the marketing discipline.

Facebook ads let advertisers reach out to their precise target audience, defined by age, location, interest and predisposition. As long as the advertising or marketing manager has been able to correctly identify their target audience, they can rely on Facebook to deliver the message to them.

Not only are there as many as twelve kinds of ad formats to help you send out a highly effective message, there are a limitless number of parameters you can leverage, when zeroing in on a target audience. Targeting in fact has now become really sophisticated, with Facebook enabling advertisers to reach out to an ever-diverse number of segments. These include niches like *recent purchase* behavior and *life events*.

3. **Economy-** Traditional advertising media is prohibitively more expensive when it comes to the cost of advertising. Facebook advertising has levelled the playing field like nothing else has. For every four dollars you spend you get to reach a thousand people. With those kinds of rates even the smallest of businesses can get their message heard loud and clear.

Gone are the days when large businesses with deep pockets and multimillion dollar advertising budgets completely elbowed out the smaller guys. A small businessman or woman can start advertising for as little as a dollar a day. Every dollar spent on Facebook advertising goes much farther than it would with Google Adwords. This is on account of the fact that you can segment and target your prospects very precisely.

4. **Ability to track performance-** With Facebook advertising what you see is what you get. This is because the advertiser is vested with the ability to precisely track performance in terms of ROI (Return on Investment) with the help of the Facebook Adverts Manager. This enables one to find out the number of times an ad is shown, the number of clicks it received from prospective customers. One can also get precise information pertaining to the cost per like, cost per click, and the cost per conversion.

5. **Social Engagement-** To not put it too delicately, Facebook is the mother of all social networks! This is what the doctor, in this case the marketer, ordered for brands to build a social and emotional connect with their target audience.

It makes eminent sense for businesses to create Facebook pages fan pages with which to engage their customers and earn their loyalty.

At the same time, it provides marketers with a great opportunity to build up their brand. Not only would the prospects and customers of the product or service being advertised, be able to obtain the required information, but leave valuable suggestions and feedback as well. Besides, they would also leave testimonials that would serve to drive up the sales.

6. **Facebook Remarketing-** You can take online advertising to the next level by leveraging the power of Facebook remarketing. Remarketing is a great concept that involves getting one's Facebook ads to show up *after* people have visited one's website or shared their email. This is also true of people who use one's app.

The beauty of this concept is that these people will get to see one's ads every time they visit other websites and social media platforms, as well on their using other apps. The ads will also appear when they watch videos or carry out online searches.

Facebook Remarketing is a very powerful way of enhancing one's business prospects. It is known to improve one's engagement rate by as much as three times and double the conversion rate. Facebook Remarketing is especially effective in ensuring call to action.

7. **More Leads Lead to More Customers-** The most important yardstick for measuring the success of any advertising campaign is the number of leads and customers it obtains. Facebook advertising wins hands down in this regards. Of course, it is important that you design the campaign intelligently, taking care to incorporate the most effective links and content.

   This is important to attract the right kind of traffic to your landing page in your website. Once you manage to create a healthy stream of traffic, you will have made yourself a great lead funnel via your Facebook advertising.

8. **Facebook Advertising Is Really Fast-** Unlike traditional advertising Facebook Advertising delivers results from the word go. You can reach thousands of your

prospects from the very first day. There isn't a faster way to attract your prospects to buy your products and services. You literally hit the deck running when it comes to conversions.

9. **Best Way to Send Traffic to Your Website-** Facebook advertising is a surefire way of sending a steady stream of traffic to your website. This is because it enables highly focused targeting, enabling you to convey traffic to your website in cost effective way.

10. **Great for Brand Building-** Facebook advertising is ideal for sustained and impactful brand building. You can really go all out to make your target audience familiar with your brand in a comprehensive manner. This will predispose them to buy your product and service at the time they do take the decision to do so.

11. **Great for Obtaining Referrals/Testimonials-** The fact Facebook is the primary social media website makes advertising on it extend you're the advantage of excellent social advocacy. If your audience relates to your ad they will share it with their friends, who in turn will share it with their, making it go viral in the process

12. **Facebook Ads Can Help You Create a Great Mailing List-** Facebook provides you with the facility of using *lead ad* forms to collect email addresses via Facebook ads. This is a great way of building a great list to aid your e mail marketing efforts.

13. **Facebook Ads Can Help Popularize Your Blog-**If blogging is your passion or you blog to promote your business, Facebook Ads can help popularize it in double quick time by sending relevant traffic there. This boost in the readership will considerably enhance your credibility among the leaders and help establish you as an authority on the subject that you blog about.

14. **You Can't Let Your Competitor Have An Edge-** The fact of the matter is that most savvy businesses, irrespective of size are already on Facebook. If you don't advertise on Facebook, not only will marketing outreach be less effective than your competitors, but you risk losing your existing clients to them as well. You simply cannot afford to not advertise on Facebook.

15. **Facebook Advertising Is for The Mobile Age-** Advertising is migrating to the mobile platform for good reason. Already 50% of all Internet users are accessing it through mobile devices. With more than 80% Facebook users accessing Facebook through mobile devices, Facebook in that sense is primed for mobile advertising. Mobile is the future. You have to take to Facebook advertising to capitalize on its compatibility with the mobile medium.

16. **Organic Facebook Marketing Is Not Enough-** While it is true that you can conscientiously try organic Facebook marketing the fact of the matter is that it is clearly not enough in today's times. You have to graduate to Facebook Advertising if you realistically want to harness the immense power of the huge Facebook outreach potential. The content that you post gets boosted by way of Facebook advertising to truly serve its purpose.

IS FACEBOOK ADVERISING RIGHT FOR YOU?

There are a number of advertising options available to marketing that range from traditional print and television to new age out-of-home and online advertising. Online advertising has gained prominence in recent years on account of its low cost, precise targeting and high return on interest.

In so far as the various online advertising platforms available to online advertisers are concerned, Google and Facebook account for the lion's share of advertising. The two behemoths have between the two of them cornered three fourth of the digital ad market, which is currently valued at more than $200 billion. So, in a sense the toss up is between these two, when it comes to creating a digital advertising plan for a business.

The reasons for choosing Facebook advertising are many, but the primary one is the fact that Facebook and its affiliated networks are the drivers of the social media revolution. This is important content and social media outreach are proving to be the most effective way to get one's targeted message out to one's target audience.

Let us delve a little deeper into this and discover why it is that Facebook is the definitive advertising medium for you-

1. **Facebook Is the World-** If Facebook would be a country, it would be the most populous one in the world. Facebook boasts of 1.49 billion accounts who generate a mind boggling 22 billion clicks a year. You cannot possibly ignore that! You have got to be on that bandwagon.

   That is because your prospective customers *are* among those account holders, what you have got to do is to figure out how to find them.

   Now you may quibble about the suitability of a social media website to promote business, but the bottomline is that businessmen and indeed businesses are represented on Facebook in extremely large numbers and it would be odd to not recognize that fact. In the past mercantile companies sent men across oceans to find access to large global markets and here you have access to a global audience of billion at the click of a mouse thanks to Facebook and its huge number of followers. Why look a gift horse in the mouth?

2. **Inexpensive Ads-** For all its humongous reach, Facebook advertising is the cheapest among all the major

advertising vehicles. The following figures make this amply clear:

S.No	Advertising Medium	Cost Of 1000 Pec
1	Newspapers	$32
2	Radio	$8
3	Cable TV	$7
4	Google AdWords	$2.75
5	LinkedIn Ads	$0.75

For every dollar you spend on a Facebook ad you get to reach four thousand people. So even if you were to spend a dollar day for a month, your message would go out to more than a hundred and twenty thousand people. What is there to not like about that?

Facebook advertising levels the playing field for businessmen and professionals with small budgets but large dreams and ambitions. You may be a great painter, but no traditional art gallery or curator is willing to support you. But you could advertise your art on Facebook and even sell it. Isn't this so liberating?

3. **Facebook Is Great for Niche Products -** Gone are the days when marketing niche products was extremely difficult on account of locating a limited target audience. That is because Facebook puts a premium on individual

expression. As a matter of fact that defines the very essence of Facebook.

There is no advertising medium that can come even close to Facebook's ability to advocate the most niche or esoteric product possible. So, if you are the caretaker of a zoo who wants to invite people to come and witness giraffes feeding, you will easily find your prospective audience on Facebook.

This unique ability of Facebook to let one fearlessly find one's niche and yet be confident of finding a lucrative market for it is so liberating to so many people who would have otherwise felt stifled.

There are for example traditional craftsmen and women in remote corners of the world who are keeping alive traditions that are hundreds and sometimes more than a thousand years old, but are now on the verge of shutting shop. Facebook advertising with its low advertising costs can help revive such businesses.

4. **Facebook Is Great for B2C (Business to Consumers)** - The USP (Unique Selling Proposition) of Facebook is the manner in which it fosters a personal connection between people. That is what makes it an ideal

platform to engage directly with consumers on a personal level and get them interested in your product.

If, for example, somebody has a small business of home-made cakes and cannot afford a steep advertising budget, all that they need to do is use Facebook ads. This will help them engage with just the kind of people who dig home-made cakes.

The thing about B2C consumers is the fact that market segmentation is of the essence. Now this is something that is right up the street of Facebook with its stellar market segmentation tools.

5. **Facebook Works Great for Small Businesses-** Small businesses that look to scale up their outreach can easily do so with the help of Facebook ads. With small startups and SOHO, Small Office and Home Office set ups becoming increasingly popular, Facebook is easily the advertising medium of choice, on account of its low cost and fantastic reach.

Not very long ago, this would not have been possible. The exorbitant marketing and advertising costs would have prevented these businesses from scaling up. With Facebook advertising millions of Davids round the world have been empowered to take on the Goliaths of the business world with confidence and assurance.

6. **Facebook Helps You Reach Out to A Mobile Audience-** More and more people are ditching the personal computer for a mobile device. Besides, a mobile device being handy is far better at engaging the attention of your target market. The fact is that Facebook and its affiliated networks Messenger and Instagram are the ten most downloaded apps in the world. Any business or individual seeking to engage with the largest number of prospects possible through their mobile device simply has to advertise on Facebook.

7. **Facebook Serves Every Belief System-** Unlike many traditional media outlets Facebook doesn't lean towards any ideology, nor does it stop an advertiser from pitching to people holding a particular political belief, political and religious affiliations. As a matter of fact, an advertiser has the liberty to and may actually benefit from zeroing in on a specific target market.

   Facebook gives you the leverage to bond with specific groups of people on an emotional level by catering to their specific needs. If a butcher specializing in kosher meat reaches out to the Jewish community on Facebook, letting them know how he respects and values their religious convictions, he sure will be able to build up a loyal clientele over time.

This wasn't always possible with traditional media where ideology did play a part sometimes and one couldn't always get one's word heard. If someone has been discriminated against on the basis of color, faith, nationality, ethnic origin and sexual orientation, they will find their voice amplified to any extent they want on Facebook.

8. **Facebook Is Great to Sell Fun and Zany Products-** If your business has to do with events, travel, entertainment, club memberships and so on advertising on Facebook is the most logical and effective way to reach out to your core audience.

This is because Facebook is the place to be for most people to connect socially, entertain themselves and have fun. People like to share with each other the places they have travelled to, the gigs that they have attended. That is where you can get them to engage with you, by providing them with exactly the service or product that they might be looking for. Position your product or service as being the one in vogue and in tune with their aspirations, and you will have them eating out of your hands.

If you were to sell sunblock lotion for pets (I am not sure that the product exists), you could sell it by advertising on

Facebook. You could even sell shoes for pets, if that was what you wanted to do!

GETTING LIKES ON FACEBOOK GROUPS

Humans are social beings. We are hardwired to seek out our communities and groups. This has its genesis in our caveman past, when being in a group provided one with safety in a dangerous world. A business, though not operating in a dangerous world certainly operates in a highly competitive world, where it needs to carve out its own space.

Now in order for it to do so, it needs friends and allies in the shape of prospects and customers. Facebook which is the number one social media is a great medium to achieve that. Any business can create a page or a group on Facebook to promote one's business and encourage users to share their thoughts and feedback on the wall. This is a great way of engaging one's prospect and customer base proactively. By its very nature a Facebook group scores substantially over a Facebook page, because the former is more participative and inclusive and fosters a feeling of belonging.

The more likes a business gets on its Facebook group, the more likely is it to retain its existing customers and convert the prospects. So, from your trying to promote your business's page, you get down to promoting your business's group, which you will agree is more inclusive and participative from the prospect's and customers' point of view.

This leads us to the all-important question about the *agenda* of the group. Is it about the business or about the target audience? Though one's objective may be to grow one's business, it cannot be an overt endeavor. You have to put your prospects' and customers' interests above yours for them to want to like your group. Say you run a travel portal. Your Facebook group is likely to receive more likes if it provides handy tips about various destinations, rather than an exhortation for your prospects to book their holidays through your portal.

On the other hand, if you restrict your messaging to only what you do, rather than what your prospects would rather do, you will not end up getting a lot of likes on your group. However, on the flip side, the percentage of the people among those that like your group who will get converted to customers will be a lot higher. This is because only the ones who are already predisposed toward your product or service will be the ones who will like your group.

For a group to be successful in its objective of receiving the maximum number of likes, it is important that it be created the right way. Here's how one might do it-

1. **Name It Right-** The name of the group decides its focus. An SUV manufacturer could create a Facebook group and call it *Off-roading Hub,* as it would want to engage with people who like to drive off-road. They would likely be interested in knowing about the off-roading capabilities of the SUV's manufactured by the company in question.

2. **Create a Close Group-** For a group to be popular and liked it needs to be exclusive and not open to everyone. A closed group will encourage its members to participate more as they know that they will be engaging only with likeminded people. Besides, they will not only feel safe from trolling of any kind, but also develop a feeling of kinship with the other group members.

3. **Create Guidelines-** A group is nothing if it is not regulated. You create a Facebook group to help you achieve certain objectives. Never lose sight of that. Lay down the guidelines that group members need to adhere to.

   If you are selling sports cars and you have created a group comprising of sports car enthusiasts, then there is no point in having motorcycle aficionados joining in. For all you know they may start bad mouthing sports cars and antagonize your core audience.

4. **Create a Forceful Persona-** You may never judge a book by its cover, but it may be able to give you a fair idea

of what to expect! In this age of extremely short attention span a glance is usually all you will be able to get from a member of your target audience and you better make that count.

Choosing an apt picture is of paramount importance. Position the picture in a manner that puts the focus on what the group is all about. If you are a content creator trying to reach out to prospective clients, you might want to use the picture of computer keyboard.

The next thing to do is to add a brief (it could be long if you so choose) but impactful description. If you run a car wash and detailing outfit, your group description might appeal to people who love their cars to death and would do anything to keep them in mint condition.

Adding tags or relevant keywords describing the objective and focus of the group will help attract the right kind of people to it. You will be auto prompted to select relevant tags so that you zero in on the most effective ones. It may be a good idea to check the number of likes the various choices have gathered

5. **Create Content-** Once the group has been created you have to hunker down and create content that resonates. Adding pictures will only add to the allure. You may also want to link your Facebook posts to your group so that your target audience is in the know of the goings on in your business. There is no point in creating a group and letting it go dormant. Your groups are like volcanoes, effective only when they are active!

6. **Get Your Blog Followers to Join-** If you already have dedicated followers from your blog you may request them to join. Being already well disposed to you and your cause, they will be excellent advocates for your cause.

7. **Promote The Group-** This is critical. You can't have a group that is not a group. If only you and your mother constitute a group that is not much of a group, is it? You simply have to make the effort to popularize the group and its cause.

   Now you have the option of inviting your Facebook friends, but the thing is that not all of them might be your target audience. Besides, they may choose not to join your group. But if there are people among your friends who you think would enhance the appeal of your group, by all means invite them.

   Alternatively, you can take the help of paid ads to give you group the much required initial push. The Facebook Ad

Manager is the place to head for with regard to this. What you also might want to try to do is to mention your group in a similar group. This may look like a cheeky thing to do, but if the rules of that group don't expressly prohibit it, you may go ahead and do this.

8. **Post on Twitter and Instagram-** Let people know of your group across social media landscapes. Reach out to your followers on Twitter and Instagram with your posts about your group. The idea is to get a critical mass of members in your group and the likes will start flowing.

When it comes to the number of likes one can possibly obtain on Facebook, it would be a good idea to look at the numbers that celebrities garner-

You would imagine that somebody like Justin Bieber with 78.7 million likes would really be top of the heap, but it is actually Cristiano Ronaldo the Portuguese soccer player with 122.1 million likes who is way ahead. In fact pop music contemporaries of Bieber like Shakira with 104.6 million likes and even Rihanna with 81 million likes are ahead of him. It might be some consolation to Bieber that he is ahead of movie star Will Smith, who has only 75.4 million likes.

HOW TO USE FACEBOOK ADS

While it is true that social media can help one reach out a large number of people for free, by choosing to not advertise and fully leverage its awesome outreach potential one may be making a huge marketing mistake.

Facebook with its humongous number of account holders who can be segmented and targeted at will has to be any marketing and advertising person's ideal scenario. In fact, it provides an ideal scenario even to novices. Now let us show you what you need to do-

1. **Get Organized-** It was mentioned earlier that social media platforms like Facebook can help you reach out organically. You have got to optimize and leverage that ability. You have got to give your Facebook page a neat and professional look. A tardy one will get up will turn off people you are trying to woo.

   Once you have the look sorted start posting quality content that will resonate with your target audience. With that part accomplished one can now look at initiating a Facebook ad campaign that will help one achieve one's outreach objectives.

2. **Get Started-** Because of the low cost of advertising and the ability to track and measure performance Facebook gives one the ability to test out a number of ads before zeroing in on the one that works perfectly for you.

   *Creating The Right Ad-*Now this is the tricky part for it relies completely on intelligent market segmentation. Facebook allows razor sharp precision with its ads. Should you want your ad to reach out to high school graduates from downtown New Jersey, you can do exactly that.

   With an ability to target anything from a dozen to a million people of a particular category, Facebook delivers bespoke advertising like nothing else does. Once you have got your segment right and the ad seems to be generating the right proportion of clicks, you can always keep the good thing going by enhancing the budget.

3. **Facebook as Part of Your Marketing Mix-** Any marketing decision has to be part of a strategy and not a shot in the dark or it will surely fail. That is equally true of Facebook, its low cost notwithstanding.

Facebook ads must have a well-defined place in one's sales funnel. This needs to be determined first. The first thing to look at is what one wants Facebook ads to accomplish-followers for one's blog, subscribers to one's eBooks or sales leads for one's products. Other factors to consider would be the kind of traffic one's website attracts and the ability to create quality content on a consistent basis.

The thing is that your Facebook Ad campaign has to be based upon achieving a certain goal. To help you achieve that goal you campaign needs to convince your prospects to act in a certain way, which becomes the *objective* of your Facebook ad campaign.

Arriving at a precise and specific target audience is the next important task at hand for a marketer who is planning a Facebook ad campaign. Now one can target one's audience according to demographics (age, gender, location, language and so on).

You can further refine the target audience by factoring in interests and predisposition. Say your target audience comprises of men between the ages of forty-five and fifty-five and the product you are promoting is running shoes with extra cushioning. Now you may want to further refine your target audience to only incorporate men between the ages of forty-five and fifty five who like to run.

The last step entails our creating an ad that you think will resonate with your target audience. Once you have the ad ready, test it first and see how it fares. If you need to tweak it, do that till you arrive at what appears to be the ideal ad. Now go ahead and run it for all its worth.

The thing about Facebook ads is that despite what it can and does regularly achieve it is quite underrated. In fact, people who should know better have not really professed its efficacy the way that they ought to.

You will find people cribbing about the fact that since everybody and their aunty is on Facebook, it has lost its relevance. Others will say that Instagram is way ahead, forgetting that Instagram is Facebook property. There are those who even rate e -mail higher.

But like they used to say in the old days-the taste of the pudding lies in its eating. If Facebook wasn't huge with its 2 billion monthly active users and its humongous advertising revenue, then tell me what is.

HACKING FACEBOOK ADS

You can make Facebook ads deliver more by deploying some clever hacks that let you leverage the awesome power of Facebook advertising to the fullest. The reason this may be critically important is the fact that many of you neither have the time nor the money to use a trial and error method to perfect your Facebook advertising campaign.

You in fact may want to hit the deck running. Here's what you might want to do to speed up things-

1. **Targeting is the Key-** In our search for clever hacks, let us not overlook the basics. You cannot completely rely on Facebook targeting options to optimally define your target audience

   You may want to use Facebook Ad Reports to help you with this. You will find it in the Ad Manager where you need to click on "Reports" located in the left side- bar. You can now click "Breakdown: None" and choose from the categories given in the list.

   The audience can be divided by-

Delivery-Age and/or gender

Actions-Conversion device and/or destination

Time-Daily or weekly

If your target audience is young people who might be accessing Facebook on their smartphones, you will be able to see if most of the people who see your ads fall into those categories. If they don't, you are obviously not going to get the right amount of ROI on your Facebook ads.

2. **Leverage the Immense Power of FOMO (Fear of Missing Out)** - This works for most products and services surprisingly well every time. Let your headline convey to your target audience that everyone in their peer group has already bought the product or service in question. This will make them feel that they might be missing out on something in life. Know the feeling when everyone you know has bought the latest iPhone and you are fretting that you don't have one?

   That is a powerful emotion to incite in your target audience. Do that.

3. **Test Your Ad Images**-A picture they say is worth a thousand words and this is certainly as true of Facebook ads. So, if you are not sure that your ads are visually appealing to your target audience, you cannot leave things to chance.

You should instead resort to A/B testing. It would be a good idea to juxtapose different versions of the ad by running a Facebook Ad Split test. In fact, also test the ad copy and placement via this test. You can easily do this by using any of the external Face ad managing tools like AdEspresso that are specially designed for A/B testing.

4. **Make An Out Of The World Value Offer-** The bottomline when it comes to your target audience reacting to your ads is to offer them something that they ardently want. Offer people a free trial period or let them know that they will get a deep discount if they choose your offering. Of course, while making these offers also let your prospects know why that they will benefit immensely if they accept your offer, as you give them something that the competition doesn't. Say you own a newspaper and offer the first month's supply free to subscribers. Also impress upon them that you have some of the best editors and journalists on your staff to ensure that they only read the highest quality content when they subscribe with you.

5. **Learn To Leverage The Ad Budget-** The thing with Facebook advertising lifetime budget is the fact that you need at least 10000 impressions to determine whether an

ad works or not. Therefore, it makes sense to allocate more money in the beginning of the campaign.

In the case of a daily budget, Facebook rarely gets to use the total budget, as the ad cannot be a total fit to your target audience's requirements. So it makes more sense to go with a larger audience budget, so that you can reach out to a bigger target audience.

6. **Study The Different Advertising Channels In Detail-**Your ad placement is determined by which channel you choose- Mobile News Feed, Instagram, Audience network, Desktop News Feed or Desktop Right Column. If you carry out some research you may discover that while mobile ads are noticed by more people, their cost of conversion may be higher. Cost per conversion is more relevant from a budgeting point of view than cost per mile or cost per click.

   You really have to try out the various ad placements to see which one leads to lowest cost per conversion in the case of your product or service.

7. **Get them with a Data Image-** What is the best way to approach a stone-cold audience who don't know a thing about you or your product? Show them a data image. One, the human brain processes images way faster than text and second raw, hard hitting data can't be argued with.

If you show a graph representing your clients' high earnings in real dollar numbers superimposed on the image of the Empire State Building you will make a point for sure.

8. **Optimize for Conversion-** Facebook deploys effective AI backed algorithms that ensure that your ads efficiently get to the people that they are supposed to reach. Therefore your focus when working on the Facebook campaign should be on zeroing in on your campaign objective. One should choose a campaign objective that approximates ones advertising goals which in most cases is sales.

9. **Use Videos-** Videos are undoubtedly the most impactful kind of content and it would be very unwise to not use them. Videos achieves a 135% more organic reach a picture does on Facebook. Now it is not always possible for companies to create videos, but they can and must use stock videos. You could choose a video based on your ad narrative on Adobe's Stock video selection.

10. **Optimal Ad Frequency-** According to psychologists your ads have to be seen three times by a person to remember it. So, try to show every ad at least three times

and possibly no more than ten times for ads appearing in the news feed, as over-exposure dulls the impact. For those appearing in the sidebar the frequency could range between 10 and 40 times.

MONETIZING YOUR FACEBOOK GROUP

Facebook has more people on board that any other social media platform. It makes eminent sense to use those numbers to your advantage to make money. A Facebook group not only lets you reach out to a larger number of people, the fact that you created the group means that you have the wherewithal to become its leader.

You own the stage, so to speak and lord over it. But the way to do it is to win over your fans loyalty. If you do that consistently over time, your fan base will only grow and make your group grow in stature and heft. You will eventually start making money on account of the growing on account of the high level of engagement with the right kind of people. How do you get to that stage? Read on-

1. **Do the Right Promotions-** If you are going to promote any product or service, it had better be something that is of genuine use to the members of the group. More than earning brownie points, it will earn you their trust and gratitude.

If your group is about running marathons, ensure that whatever you promote on your website is relevant to that main topic. The key to endearing yourself to the group is to go out of your way to ensure that the product or service that you promote to the group is of stellar quality that provides the group members with value. If you pull a fast one on them and purvey anything that is not up to their expectations, you can forget achieving anything worthwhile with that group.

2. **Attract Traffic-** You can leverage your Facebook groups to leverage traffic to your website, blog, or YouTube channel. The way to do this is by posting their links in your Facebook group along with a short description about their contents. It would be a good idea to incorporate a call-to-action that would have the people view the content. They may in turn share it with other groups or even in their personal timelines.

   If you get a fair amount of traffic to your various sites, you will end up earning from it.

3. **Paid Web Ticket Events-** You can hold a paid web ticket event that makes a lot of sense to your group members and offer them an early bird discount. Your group members will want in early because you are providing them with great value.

Say your group is all about home security and you hold a paid web ticket about- *"How to tackle armed intruders in your home with what you have got?"* What's there to not like about that for such a group. Sure, they will want to avail of the early bird discount.

4. **Get a Relevant Business to Advertise in the Group-** You can identify businesses that are able to provide quality products or services to your group members and let them advertise in the group. In the case of a marathon runners' group, you can let manufacturers of running shoes advertise. The way to facilitate this is by pinning their post to the top of the group, complete with an updated cover photo of the group indicating the advertiser as a sponsor or partner.

5. **Use Affiliate Marketing Links-** The thing is that each Facebook group caters to a niche and this is something that appeals to affiliate marketers. There will be e commerce websites that sell products affiliated to that interests of the group. You can enter into an affiliate marketing tie up with these websites. Every time one of your group members clicks on a link taking them to the

affiliated e commerce site and they end up buying, you will get a percentage of the sale value.

6. **Advertise Your Own Products or Services-** As you have taken all the trouble to create the group and grow it you can surely pin details of your own products and services to the top of the group. Besides, this kind of advertising will cost you nothing and you will be able to convert customers from group members who are already well disposed toward you.

While it is a great idea to go ahead and try to monetize your Facebook group, the fact of the matter is that it is not as straight forwards it sounds. The very purpose behind creating a closed Facebook group is to encourage exclusivity. You are creating a safe enclave for likeminded people where they can freely and frankly exchange views and ideas without worrying about getting spammed or pressured by marketers.

It will take a great deal of sincere content creation and looking out for the core interests of the group for anyone to build credibility and loyalty. To introduce branding and positioning of one's products and services no matter how subtly done will always be fraught with the risk of antagonizing one's core audience.

Holding a group together, as anyone would know, is always a very tenuous affair. If you start to market a brand, you will most likely raise the hackles of certain members of the group. How you manage that is a test of your dexterity and marketing ability.

Marketing at its very core is need fulfilment. You will need to convince the group that mentioning your product or services is actually an outcome of your perfect understanding of their needs. If you can convey that sincerely, you will have an ace up your sleeves, as they will themselves willingly buy your products and services.

GROWING YOUR FACEBOOK FOLLOWING

The strength of your Facebook following is what is going to determine the success of your Facebook marketing strategy. If you are on Facebook to promote your business and not just socialize with family and friends, you have to take a professional approach toward growing your Facebook following. Any content that you may create could factor in the following-

1. **Study and Understand Your Market-** You have got to have a firm handle on who constitutes your market. This will let you have a fair idea of who among the huge number of Facebook members would likely be interested in your products and services.

   This will impact upon the kind of content that you might want to create and forcefully advocate to the target market. The Facebook Audience Insight tool could help you with identifying the precisely right kind of target audience. You can begin by finding the Create Audience section inside Facebook Audience Insights. Over there you have the facility of inputting the country and region your target market corresponds with.

Next go to the Interests section and identify your area of interest say running shoes. Now analyze the audience data that comes up and leverage the data to make appropriate adjustments to your audience in the Create Audience section. You can refine your target audience to quite an extent based on the many demographic data that are available to you. For instance in the case of rubbing shoes, age of the audience would be a vital demographic to consider.

2. **Niche Down-** It is not enough to know the broad segment your target market occupies. You have got to find out the specific interests of your target audience, so that your content is able to address their concerns with pinpoint accuracy. Again the additional audience tool within Facebook Audience Insights can help you with this.

It would for instance really help if you would know what wearers of running shoes look at when buying one-comfort, durability or price? The more information that you possess about the disposition of your target audience the more your content will resonate with them.

3. **Create Content That Serves the Niche Well-** Now that you have a pretty good idea of what your specific target niche wants, create tailored content that gives them exactly that. You should also leverage the power of relevant images. A picture prominently highlighting the joy of running would surely resonate with a Facebook group dedicated to running. The posts themselves should delve into what interests the group in a finely nuanced and genuine way.

For people who constitute a marathoners' segment, posts about nutrition and the importance of keeping oneself hydrated during long distance runs would surely interest people. It would be best to not flaunt your brand for that may put people off your content.

Instead make the copy spry and interesting and replete with information. You can use emojis to good effect to spruce up the content. Try to engage the target audience by including a call to action. You could for instance put a question to the marathon runners' group-"How many of you know the about the origin of the marathon race?"

4. **Help the Post Along With A Little Boost-** It is all very well to grow your Facebook audience organically, but a little paid boost is probably just what the doctor added to give you quicker traction. If you spend a handful of dollars to boost the post to reach more of your carefully segmented target audience, you would be doing your cause more than a bit of a favor.

5. **Perfect the Art of Creating Posts That Resonate-** You have got to get good at identifying the types of posts that lead to intense engagement. If some post has gone down exceedingly well with your target audience, it is a no brainer that you should try to replicate its success by incorporating its importance in the next one.

   If for instance a chiropractor gives out tips about neck care in a certain format that is immensely liked by a large number of people, it might make sense to put up another post with regards to tips about back care.

6. **Learn To Use Hooks That Work-** There are a few things that are proven response generating hooks, when it comes to attracting one's target audience to engage with one's post. These include-
-Questions
-Pictures
-Fill in the blanks
-Contests
-Videos

7. **Patience Is a Virtue-** You can't hope to become a social media marketing genius within days of starting out. You have got to win over your target audience by creating content consistently over a long period of time and nurturing your relationship with them.

This may not show results immediately, but your target audience would have made a mental note somewhere about your offerings. When the time is right, they will approach you. But in the meantime, you have to carry on creating content and working on building and maintaining your relationships with the target audience.

If you have been consistently putting out topical and highly relevant information about marathons and marathoners which is highly valued by those kind of people, you may not immediately see them buying your running shoes. But with time, once their old shoes need replacement, they would most likely consider buying from you their most natural choice.

8. **Keep Your Content Real and Relatable-** Don't appear desperate for sales. Easy does it has to be a motto here, as you don't want your most ardent followers to be turned off.

So even if there is no immediate sign of revenue, don't panic. Focus on serving the interests of your target audience well and things will slowly pan out well for you. A post a day is quite fine in the beginning. You don't want your potential fans to think that you are stalking them.

Engage with them organically and enjoy the process. Rome wasn't built in a day. You will get to where you want if you focus on providing value consistently over a period of time.

9. **Keep Creating High Quality Content-** There can be no half measures if you want to create a loyal and credible Facebook fan following. You have got

to be disciplined and draw up a posting schedule for out of sight is not only out of mind, it also conveys the impression that you are not reliable.

The important thing is to draw up a schedule and follow it religiously. There really should be no compromise there.

10. **Tracking-** Remember I told you that Facebook marketing is serious business and you have got to take it seriously? Well, that does not only include identifying the target audience, creating posts for them with a set schedule and engaging with them. It also includes taking stock of how successful you have been. After all that's the whole point of all the trouble that you have taken.

You could do it once a month and see what you have got yourself for all your hard work and efforts. If you have done very well, congratulations, if you haven't, identify where you slipped and take corrective action.

The thing about growing your Facebook following is the fact that you are not to intimidate your reader but make friends with them. Create content that they would love to share. If you are teaching them how to make money by trading on the stock market, explain things in a user-friendly manner like you would to a friend. Don't overwhelm them with technical jargon. If you are showing off, you are not catering to their need of learning how to invest. You genuinely teach them how to invest in shares and make a profit, they will spread the word and traffic will grow for your content.

Carry out a deep study of your followers and find out what type of content that they really dig and make viral. See if you can provide them something along those lines on a regular basis. If you do manage to do that you are on your way to growing your followers to an unprecedented level.

Another great way of having followers join you by the hordes is to tell an emotional story. Hard facts and statistics often faze people, but a story that connects at a human level never fails. In fact, it resonates across nationalities and cultures.

Even if your aim is to popularize your brand, if you weave a story around it, you will go far. Say you sell vegetables and are trying to gain followers on Facebook. If you make a post where you tell them how you use only organic fertilizer produced in the compost pit that is maintained by the inmates of the local prison as part of their rehabilitation program to grow the vegetables.

What would otherwise have been a mere vegetable business now turns into something noble as people will root for you and your business. The thing to remember is that the story has to be genuine and not contrived or it will not resonate with the target audience. Not only do people communicate with stories and love to hear them; they also love to share them.

You also need to have a fair understanding of the kind of content that Facebook takes to. For instance, posts with captions and pictures or captions and links are liked more than just a linked website page or photo.

Also, you cannot be living in an ivory tower where you occasionally put out content and expect the world to follow your posts. You have got to be interactive and follow people back. You should really be proactive and interact with people who follow pages similar to yours. Get them over to your side.

It is also important that you are able to develop a feeling of kinship with your followers. Try to strike a personal and friendly note with your followers. This is how you will create loyalty. People would rather relate to another flesh and bone individual than to a brand.

It is only through you the person that they will get to know your brand. Identify what bothers them and try to provide a solution and you will have them profess their loyalty to you.

Remember loyal and engaged followers are more important than a massive number of followers who actually don't empathize with you at all.

You have got to remember that it is not how many followers you have but who you have that matters. There are any number of scammers who will sell you fake followers, but what value will they bring you? It doesn't matter if you don't have too many followers to start with, you can nurture them and grow them. After all, the journey of a thousand steps began with a single step.

AUTOMATING FACEBOOK INCOME

They say that you are really making money when you do that while you are sleeping! Humongous and gargantuan are the words that come to mind when you think of the billions of users that Facebook boasts of. It won't be remiss to imagine that this could be leveraged to earn oneself a neat regular income. Creating a large fan base of course is the very first step. Next, you could have in place an automatic scheduling system that puts content in front of your target audience. You can look ahead to generating automated income thanks to your Facebook highly popular content!

The thing is no matter how hard you work, you can only accomplish a finite amount of output and consequently earn finite amount of income. But surely, we deserve a better life than that and far more income. The only way you can do it is if you can somehow automate some of the work that you do so that it happens relentlessly on its own even if you are enjoying some well-deserved leisure time. Here's how you might do it with Faccbook-

1. **Facebook Ads plus dropshipping-** What you are required to do over here is that you may run a Facebook ad campaign targeting a certain segment of the audience with the intention of guiding people to the landing page of a website that serves as the order page of your product. The customers can place their orders there and the onus of delivering the product is on the dropshipper. There is very little risk as you don't need to maintain an inventory. You only risk the money that you invest in the paid ads and if you don't get enough orders you may end up losing money.

2. **Use Hootsuite-** Hootsuite automates the posting process reaching out to a calibrated pre-selected audience, thereby considerably speeding up the engagement process and ultimately leading to enhanced automation.

3. **99 Dollar Social-**This handy tool will not only find great topical content for you, but also create stellar customized posts for you complete with hash tags and great imagery. It completely automates your Facebook posting on a daily basis, all seven days of the week setting you on the path to automating your Facebook income.

4. **Use Facebook to Send Traffic to Blog or Storefront-** If you have a huge number of fans on Facebook you can seek to send them to your monetized blog and earn revenue from Google Ad Sense.

5. **Tie Up With Amazon-** Your Facebook fans could surely be encouraged to buy products from the world's greatest online retailer with millions of products on offer. All that you need to do is to sign up for the Amazon affiliate program through Amazon Associates. They will provide you with an affiliate link that you can use to promote their products to your Facebook fans. Surely a win win situation for everyone, if there ever was one.

6. **A Facebook App Store-** You can exercise the option of setting up a store in a tab app by using services like Shopify. This will allow you to have a storefront on Facebook that your followers can use to shop creating an automated source of income for you.

The key to leveraging the awesome reach of Facebook in a manner that makes automation of income with Facebook's help possible is to understand the limit of growing your fan base organically. You do seriously need to think of investing some money to take matters to another level.

As a matter of fact you need to take a series of steps. You have got to make an effort to promote your posts. This will enable you to send more people to your website and thereby make more sales conversions.

You can also get your tab installed and increase engagement with its help. You can endeavor to reach the right demographic of people and stage an event for those people where they receive an offer they cannot refuse. Use video posts extensively to grab attention, so as to collect leads for your business.

The above steps may not seem like they are ushering in total automation of your Facebook income, but they are definitely sending you in that direction by streamlining your outreach efforts and scaling them up. Completely automating your Facebook income was never going to happen overnight. You have got to make it happen patiently over time. It may seem like a lot of trouble, but it is well worth it.

Facebook advertising if leveraged properly can make life so much easier. Not only could one grow and scale up any business one likes, one could do so in a manner where not a minute goes to waste. One could grow one's business, generate wealth and still have time for leisure.

All of this is not a pipe dream, but a reality which so many people are living. People everywhere have taken to the digital way of life as it shows them a path which is so much different and better than the conventional 9 am to 5pm, brick and mortar grind that the world was used to. Platforms like Facebook have liberated people from the shackles of conformity and ordinary living. People now dare to dream because they know that they possess the wherewithal to achieve these.

Platforms like Facebook have played a crucial role in unleashing the creative energies of millions possibly billons of people around the world. This can only augur extremely well for the world in the times ahead. Of course, Facebook too is evolving all the time with technological developments adding to its bouquet offerings.

While there is no doubt about the fact that Facebook is one of the greatest marketing and advertising platforms ever, it is important that one understands it well to be able to fully leverage its full power. That means that marketers and advertisers would have their tasks cut out in trying to update themselves with the newest offerings from the number one social media site in the word.

We live in the midst of the most exciting technological revolution that has changed the destiny of the human race in the shortest period of time and in the most profound way possible. Facebook of course has been one of the primary drivers of this revolution and impacts upon the life of most of humanity. Interesting times lie ahead for all of us and Facebook.